Rer.

The Fuck You Are

Are

Steps you can take on the path to finding yourself again.

ALEXIAN HEWITT

Table of Contents

WHO ARE YOU?

A few days ago, a friend of mine made a post asking, *"have you ever been stuck?"*

It struck me because that is exactly how I was feeling, then it dawned on me, Haven't we all? I think we have all been there, in that place where we felt stuck or felt as though we have lost ourselves or just forgotten who we once were. Quite often, we lose sight of the things that make us who we are -our core values- or who we envisioned ourselves to be, we lose sight of what we believe in, we lose our voices, our perspective, and eventually, ourselves. Anything can make us lose ourselves; it is one of the easiest things to do because it takes little to no effort at all.

Who are you? Who you are is a combination of so many different things, your experiences, your circumstances, your beliefs… basically everything relating to you; everything you already know about yourself, as well as the things that you have yet to discover. A part of what makes you who you are, are the things that drive you, your core values, your interests, et al. These things make up your individuality. For me, I've always been a very passionate person; I have a deep appreciation for life. I learnt to be independent from a tender age, always in survival mode, fending for myself, I was forced to be a strong individual and that grew with me. My circumstances drove me; it made me hungry for success. I say this to say, these things, my passion for life and drive for success, helped to make me who I was. As I grew, I evolved; I started having different interests, I developed passions for many different things, I fostered my own opinions and established my own perspective and outlook on life.

Basically, I became *ME.*

For a long time, I had lost myself. I lost touch of who I was, completely, and I forgot what I was about, what I stood for, what I believed in. I was just going with the flow. And even worse, I was okay with it. When I met my current partner, I lost my individuality, unintentionally so. I became so comfortable that I created a nest. For a while I was no longer interested in my dreams. My goals and aspirations were distant memories, I was no longer interested in going out to meet new people and form new experiences because all my focus was on my new relationship.

Then one day I woke up and I did not recognize myself anymore, one of the worst possible feelings. I was not the same passionate person who was excited about life anymore; I was not doing all the things that made me happy- the things that I once loved were now just distant memories. I did not have any drive, no edge, I was no longer hungry for success and it dawned on me. I was not me; I did not know who the fuck I was, but it sure as hell was not me. I had lost myself. The sad truth took a while to settle in, and then came the frustration. I became angry with myself and with my partner, then I was sad, honestly, I was just a mess! I had no idea what to do with myself and one day it struck me, I knew what I needed to do, it became clear as day almost as if someone was speaking to me.

I needed to remember Who The Fuck I was.

There are four simple steps that I took that helped me do just that. In this book I talk about these four simple steps that you must take on your path to finding yourself again.

Lose Yourself To Find Yourself

Losing yourself is probably one of the easiest things to do, because it takes little to no effort. Finding yourself again is the hard part. Quite simply put, to 'lose' oneself is to become completely absorbed when doing something; so much so that one's sense of self and one's sense of time passing are temporarily non-existent.

Anything can cause you to lose yourself; it could be a job/career that you spend too much time investing in, so you miss out on spending quality time on other aspects of your life. You miss out on doing the things that make you who you are, the things that make you happy. And there shouldn't be just one thing that makes you who you are or that makes you happy, there must be a bunch of little things that combine to make you an individual. So sure, your job might be one of the things that make you happy, but it should not be the only thing and therefore, you must make time for the other things that make you happy; you must create a balance. When you aren't at work engage in other things that you love doing, such as, painting maybe or dancing, hanging out with friends and family; whatever it is, just make sure you are creating the right balance between work and the other parts of your life, so you don't lose sight of who you are.

Becoming Parents; There is this notion that when you become a mother, you have to put your life on hold because you are now responsible for someone else's life. One word: *bullshit.*

It's all about creating a balance that works for you, but you should never have to give up your own life or happiness. Your happiness should never be at the expense of someone else's happiness. In fact, I believe it's the opposite, when mommy is happy and is her best self then she can create a happy loving environment for her kids. Still make time to do the things that you enjoyed doing before becoming a parent. This is one of the most common ways to lose yourself, because your children become the only thing you focus on, you forget about your own life, you forget that you even had a life before you gave birth.

A Relationship/Marriage; Persons tend to get tunnel vision when a relationship is new, meaning they start solely focusing on the relationship and their partner. While this is a good thing, it can also be a recipe for disaster. It is okay to want to spend lots of time with your beau or your girl and this is often the case in new relationships. What is not okay though, is when you start neglecting other aspects of your life in the process. There should always be a balance. Why do we stop trying once we find someone? You should still dress up and go out to have drinks. Have dates with friends. Still do all the things that you loved to do before you met your partner, still have a life! Have your own thing going on. When you stop, not only do you become unattractive to yourself, but also to your partner, because you've stopped doing all the things that made you the amazing person you are. But also, you no longer do the things that once gave you joy... you have neglected your friends so now you don't have a social life; you are no longer passionate about life. You have lost yourself.

Whatever the case may be; suddenly you stop doing the things that once gave you joy and purpose. And then one day, one day you wake up and you realize you are not excited about your life, hell sometimes you may not even want to wake up or get out of bed. I call this the dark place. This feeling of being lost sends you into a state of panic which lowers your frequency.

The irony though, is that you must lose yourself in order to find yourself, losing yourself is a part of the process of self-growth. If you feel lost, recognize that this is the process and you're on your journey; to explore, to learn, to evolve. Self-discovery requires getting lost. That's how we learn about ourselves, who we are, what we are meant to be, who we're intended to meet, what we're meant to learn from them, and where we're destined to go. That is how we become.

LOST

IN A RUT

You may feel as though you're stuck in a state where you barely or don't even recognize yourself, you're just going through the motions of your life, day after day after day. Each day seemingly less bearable than the last, everyday monotonous and predictable, and your passion for life quickly wanes as a result. One day you are excited about life and hungry for everything life has to offer, and then you wake up years later barely even able to recognize yourself.

You've lost yourself and this state that you are currently in is known as a rut. To be in a rut is to be stuck in a habit or course of action, especially a boring one.

Your first step towards getting out of a rut is to acknowledge that you are in one. This first step requires introspection; Introspection is such a very important and necessary thing. You need to able to look within yourself and see for yourself that you are stuck and be willing to do something about it, until you are willing to look at yourself and admit that "okay, I am stuck, I am in a place in my life where I don't want to be, I am in a place in my life where I don't even recognize myself anymore" you will stay stuck.

"Our lives improve only when we take chances and the first and most difficult risk, we can take is to be honest with ourselves." ~Walter Anderson

Recently I realized I was exactly at this point in my life, where I had lost myself, I looked in the mirror and I no longer recognized the person that was staring back, I was in a rut…I was just going through the motions of life one monotonous day after another. But the key thing to note is I 'realized' that I was at this point in my life and I decided to do something about it. Well truthfully, first I became extremely depressed, but after that I decided to do something about it. This is what I did…

MY WHY

Figure out your WHY

I heard someone say something and it resonated with me, so much so that I began to give it some serious thought. He said "there was something missing in this world, a void that God needed you to fill when he created you"

And I sat down, and I started to think to myself; What void did God need me to fill? Why did he create me? What is my purpose?

I struggled with figuring out my why for the longest time. Therefore, this was a very difficult activity for me. I had asked myself these same questions multiple times before and I got nowhere with the answers. But I completed the four steps in this book, and I asked myself these same questions again once I was through. One particular morning, while I was praying it came to me clear as day. God created me to serve as a beacon for others. A source of light or inspiration; a guide.

Now, this did not come as a surprise to me, because I've always had a need to try and help others, to try and steer them in the right direction, to help them to ultimately figure things out. To guide and advise them. To enlighten and encourage. These are all things that I found myself always doing, whether it was subconsciously or consciously. And I was good at it! Suddenly it all made sense.

Now prior to this I had started to realize that Persons would come to me for advice for just about anything. There are people who genuinely value my opinion on different things. I had people who have reached out to me saying I inspired and motivated them. It gave me such gratification. For a time, I started noticing that I was surrounded by people who always needed my help, emotionally, or persons who were going through dark periods in their lives. I had begun to wonder why I was attracting this kind of energy. What was I thinking about or doing that was manifesting these particular people who needed emotional help? It came to a point where it was completely draining my own energy because I was pouring from an empty cup.

I did not understand it. I did not know at the time that I was created to be a beacon for others, "a source of light" for those who were going through dark times. I was struggling with my own negative feelings of unworthiness, like who do I think I am? giving advice to people or encouraging others. I felt unworthy, unloved, misjudged and a bunch of other negative feelings.

Before I could step into my purpose, I needed to fill my own cup; I needed to find myself, find out who I was at my core, my reason for being here. I needed to find myself first before I could be a beacon to others.

What is your why? What void did God need you to fill when he created you?

Your "Why" has a big part to do with who you are ultimately.

In this book I will share with you the four simple steps that I took on my journey to finding myself. It's not a magical book, you will definitely have to do the work in order to find yourself this is merely a guide.

After you have completed the four steps, you can ask yourselves these questions: What is my why? What void did God need me to fill when he created me?

_____

_____

_____

_____

_____

_____

STEP 1- MAKE A LIST

TAP INTO YOUR MEMORY

I did some serious soul searching. I wrote a list of all the things I used to enjoy doing before this point in my life... The things that made me happy, I sat down, and I had to think hard about the things that I once loved and then I wrote a list. I reflected on when I was the happiest in my life.

Two very important questions I asked myself when I was doing this were:

"When am I the happiest?"

"What do I do with the most enthusiasm?"
This part was extremely hard for me personally because I struggled to remember the things that made me happy, but eventually I completed my list.

That person you are when you are your happiest, that is the person you want to be, that's who you should always be; your truest, most genuine, happiest self, your best self. **Maya Angelou once said, "There is no greater agony than bearing an untold story inside you."** You can't afford to waste an entire lifetime not fulfilling your purpose and becoming who you were meant to be.

Now I challenge you to make a list; take a moment to remember a time before you were in a rut. These are some of the questions you can think about when you are making your list: What were you excited about? What were some of the things that you were looking forward to doing? What are some of the things you enjoyed doing? What were some of your plans for your life? Think about these questions, take as much time as you need but it's very important that you are honest with yourself while doing this activity. I want you to write down the first things that come to your mind when you hear or read these questions.

When you're through with this activity I need you to write down your goals, aspirations and dreams; the things that you want to accomplish, write down what you had always envisioned for your life. You can also create a vision board. The reason for this is because waking up and looking at the things that you want or hope to accomplish every day really does motivate you and most importantly, it reminds you who you want to

be, so that it is harder to lose yourself again,

even if you start to settle back into your

comfort zone.

Now I challenge you to make a list; take a

moment to remember a time before you were

in a rut. These are some of the questions you

can think about when you are making your

list: What were you excited about? What are

some of the things that you were looking

forward to doing? What are some of the

things you enjoyed doing? What were some of

your plans for your life?

Think about these questions, take as much

time as you need but it"s very important that

you are honest with yourself while doing this

activity. I want you to write down the first

things that come to your mind when you hear

or read these questions.

_____

_____

_____

_____

_____

When you are through with this activity, I

need you to also write down your goals,

aspirations, and dreams; the things that you

want to accomplish, write down what you

had always envisioned for your life.

_____

_____

_____

_____

_____

_____

I also recommend creating a vision board. The

reason for this is because waking up and

looking at the things that you want or hope to accomplish every day really does motivate you, and most importantly it reminds you. This makes it harder to lose yourself again, even if you start to settle back into your comfort zone.

STEP 2- CREATE A LIFE THAT YOU'RE EXCITED ABOUT

DO THINGS THAT MAKE YOU WANT TO JUMP

OUT OF BED EVERY DAY

After I wrote my list, I made it a point of duty to do at least two of those things every day. It took a lot of effort because I was forcing myself to come out of the comfortable bubble that I had created for myself. Let me tell you, it was hard, but it felt great!

Now that you have made your list, this is what I want you to do: Stop asking permission to live your life. Do everything and anything that makes you happy. Also do things that make you feel good, engage in things that are improving your self-development every day. Here is what I want you to do next; GET UP off that couch or crawl out of that bed and GO DO those things that you wrote down in chapter three, as well as, trying something new at least once a week. Whatever it is, it does not have to be anything elaborate! If you like to run, Get your sneakers, and go run on the beach or go out for an early morning run!! If you like to go out and socialize, text your friends and meet up! What are you waiting for? Take that dance class!! Try a new dish! Visit that place you have always wanted to go! Whatever it is, create a life for yourself that you enjoy, one that makes you excited to jump out of bed and get your day started.

Once you start doing the things you love, appreciating and having a passion for life will come at default. And ultimately, when you are happy and excited about life, it radiates a positive energy and atmosphere, and that will

reflect in your life. It's the law of attraction.

STEP 3: TAP INTO YOUR INNERMOST SELF

SELF-REFLECTION

A big part of finding yourself includes understanding who you are. One way to do this is through self-reflection. You will realize it is difficult to really know yourself until you have spent time thinking about the things that matter the most to you.

If you don't truly understand who you are, what you stand for, what your core values are, what your interests are, what your likes and dislikes are, how can you find yourself? You must go through the process of taking time to get to know yourself. To understand and find out what makes you who you are. Through self-reflection, you are able to do that.

Self-reflection is a process through which your understanding of who you are grows, and you learn what your core values are and why you think and act the way you do. It is a form of personal assessment that helps you to bring your life into alignment with what and who you desire to become.

It is at this point that true discovery happens, it is where we are most raw and vulnerable, and it is where most of the hard work takes place. You can't find yourself until you discover your true self.

This stage in finding yourself can be very difficult as this is a time when you allow yourself to be completely vulnerable so that you can tap into your innermost self to find who you really are. And being open and vulnerable, even to ourselves, can be a very uncomfortable thing for a lot of us

Losing yourself can have you feeling as though you have been asleep for years, but it's never too late to get in touch with your inner self. This inner power that you are bound to discover will allow you to live a life with meaning and purpose, a life that makes you happy.

Many people do not know themselves and they live a life never finding out because it's too uncomfortable to be in touch with their own thoughts, having their every flaw staring back at them is terrifying. But until you get in touch with your inner self, do some self-evaluation and become completely truthful with yourself, you will never be able to see every facet of your life.

You must learn the art of accessing and understanding your thoughts. That's the only way you'll be able to discover your true essence, your potential, and everything you have to offer.

Every one of us has an inner self. That inner self has tons of amazing qualities, but it is hidden deep down inside, and it is up to you to let it out by tapping into it. Acknowledge that self that is deep inside and let it become you, because it is you.

STEP 4: RE LEARN WHO YOU ARE

DATE YOURSELF

Oftentimes we get so caught up in being who others say we're supposed to be or want us to be, that we silence our own desires to make everyone else happy. We choose a life based on what others think is best for us. You may have wanted to become a singer, but your dad thought it would be best if you became a Doctor, so you became a doctor, you may have wanted to travel the world, but you had children and you were told it's all about your children now, so you forgot about traveling. You may have always wanted to become an actor or actress. but you were told it is impossible to make it in the movie industry, so again, you buried your dreams, whatever it may have been. These are all examples of how we stifle who we are or our dreams to "do what's best" or to make others happy. It is so easy to get caught up and lose sight of what our core values are, our needs and our desires. Eventually, we lose ourselves because we have been so caught up in projections of who we are.

There is a reason God designed each of us individually, with our own personalities, our own bodies, and our own minds. It is so we would be able to exercise free will and choose a life for ourselves; doing the things that we want to do with our lives, to lead a life that makes us happy, to fulfill our individual purposes. I'm here to tell you today that you can, and you should!

Take time to get to know you again. The REAL you, not the version of you that society prefers, or the version of that your parents think you should be. Get to know the REAL you again. Spend as much time alone, doing things that you enjoy doing, things that YOU love. It could be reading a book, writing a poem, playing games, watching funny videos, cooking, dancing in your mirror, whatever it is. Date yourself. Get to know yourself; your likes, your dislikes, your beliefs, and values- what matters the most to you. Get to know your strengths and weaknesses. Get to know your body - your preferences and tastes.

Figure out who you are alone, without a

boyfriend, without a job, without friends,

without kids. Ask yourself: who am I? Who

would I be without this job? Who would I be

if I were not his wife? Who would I be if I

were not a mother? And spend time trying to

figure it out. Take yourself out on dinner

dates, go see a movie. Whatever it is that you

like doing with others, try doing it by

yourself. Take notice of how you are when

you are not around anyone else to be judged,

assessed, or criticized. This is your truest self;

who you are alone when you think no one

else is watching. That is when you let down

your hair and let go.

SUMMARY OF KEY POINTS

- You must lose yourself to find yourself...self-discovery requires getting lost.
- Figure out your why.
- Make a list of all the things that made you happy before you lost yourself
- Create a life that you are excited about...do things that make you want to jump out of bed every day
- Tap into your innermost self you must discover your true self to find who you are
- Re learn who you are; take the time to get to know the REAL you

EPILOGUE

I hope by now you have started on your journey to re-discovering or to discovering who you are. I hope these four simple steps that I took on my journey to finding myself again will be useful on your journey to finding yourself. You must understand that finding yourself will require vulnerability and honesty. You must be honest with yourself on your path to finding who you are.

Made in the USA
Middletown, DE
06 May 2023

29636252R00033